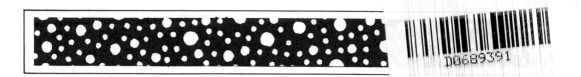

WILD ABOUT MUFFINS

BY ANGELA CLUBB

BARRON'S

New York • London • Toronto • Sydney

First U.S. edition published 1985 by
Barron's Educational Series, Inc.

Published by arrangement with Clarke Irwin (1983), Inc.

Copyright © 1982 by Angela Clubb

The title of the Canadian edition is *Mad About Muffins.*

All inquiries should be addressed to:
Barron's Educational Series, Inc.
250 Wireless Boulevard
Hauppauge, New York 11788

Library of Congress No. 84-28243

International Standard Book No. 0-8120-2910-1

Library of Congress Cataloging in Publication Data
Clubb, Angela.
    Wild about muffins.

    Includes index.
    1. Muffins. I. Title.
TX769.C56 1985   641.8'15   84-28243
ISBN 0-8120-2910-1

Design by Milton Glaser Inc.
Color photographs by Karen Leeds
Helga Weinrib, food stylist
Linda Peacock, prop stylist

PRINTED IN HONG KONG

1 2 3   4 9 0   9 8 7

Not for sale in Canada

CONTENTS

This book is dedicated to all muffin lovers.

INTRODUCTION

T*he muffin, once called a "little muff"—to keep the hands warm—has long been a favorite. Now, however, you are no longer restricted to the humble little bran muffin. Buckwheat, wheat germ, nuts, dried fruits, and yogurt are widely available and make interesting and nourishing ingredients. Try serving muffins as an alternative to dinner rolls or bread; encourage your children to enjoy them as snacks.*

I am indebted to my family and friends who assisted me by consuming most of the test muffins. My thanks also to Susan Walker for her ideas and encouragement.

A NOTE ABOUT METRICATION

All recipes in this book are given in both customary and metric measures. The metric measures are not exact equivalents to the customary counterparts, but have been rounded off to standard metric units. On the pages that follow, we've also included conversion tables to help cooks in England and Australia. Refer to these tables should you prefer to use Imperial or Australian measures.

CONVERSION TABLES

The weights and measures in the lists of ingredients and cooking instructions for each recipe are in both U.S. and metric units.

LIQUID MEASURES

The Imperial cup is considerably larger than the U.S. cup. Use the following table to convert to Imperial liquid units.

AMERICAN CUP (in book)	IMPERIAL CUP (adjusts to)
¼ cup	4 tablespoons
⅓ cup	5 tablespoons
½ cup	8 tablespoons
⅔ cup	¼ pint
¾ cup	¼ pint + 2 tablespoons
1 cup	¼ pint + 6 tablespoons
1¼ cups	½ pint
1½ cups	½ pint + 4 tablespoons
2 cups	¾ pint
2½ cups	1 pint
3 cups	1½ pints
4 cups	1½ pints + 4 tablespoons
5 cups	2 pints

Note: The Australian and Canadian cup measures 250 mL and is only slightly larger than the U.S. cup, which is 236 mL. Cooks in Australia and Canada can follow the exact measurements given in the recipes, using either the U.S. or metric measures.

SOLID MEASURES

British and Australian cooks measure more items by weight.
Here are approximate equivalents for basic items in the book.

	U.S. Customary	Imperial
Apples (peeled and sliced or diced)	1 cup	4 oz.
	3 cups	1 lb.
Bran	1 cup	2 oz.
Butter	1 tablespoon	½ oz.
	¼ cup	2 oz.
	½ cup	4 oz.
	1 cup	8 oz.
Cheese (grated)	½ cup	2 oz.
Cornmeal	1 cup	6 oz.
Flour (sifted)	¼ cup	1¼ oz.
	½ cup	2½ oz.
	1 cup	5 oz.
	1½ cups	7½ oz.
	2 cups	10 oz.
Fresh fruit (berries)	1 cup	8 oz.
Herbs (fresh, chopped)	¼ cup	¼ oz.
Nuts (chopped)	¼ cup	1 oz.
	½ cup	2 oz.
	1 cup	4 oz.
Raisins (sultanas)	¼ cup	1½ oz.
	½ cup	3 oz.
	1 cup	6 oz.
Sugar (granulated/brown)	¼ cup	1¾ oz.
	½ cup	3 oz.
	1 cup	6½ oz.
Vegetables, Chopped (zucchini, onions, carrots, celery)	½ cup	2 oz.
	1 cup	4 oz.
Wheat Germ/Bran Cereal	½ cup	1½ oz.
	1 cup	3 oz.

OVEN TEMPERATURES

British cooks should use the following settings.

Gas Mark	¼	2	4	6	8
Fahrenheit	225	300	350	400	450
Celsius	107	150	178	205	233

A NOTE ABOUT INGREDIENTS

The names for ingredients used in this book are terms that will be familiar to U.S. and Canadian cooks. For cooks in England and Australia, be aware of the following:

All-purpose flour = Plain flour
Semi-sweet chocolate = Plain chocolate
Brown sugar = Soft brown sugar
Baking soda = Bicarbonate of soda
Molasses is closest to treacle

SIMPLE STEP-BY-STEP GUIDE

M*uffins can be prepared within 10 to 20 minutes and baked in 20 to 25 minutes using these simple steps:*

1.   Preheat oven. *Most muffins are best when baked at 400°F (200°C). Place oven rack in the middle. Reduce temperature by 25°F (40°C) for a dark nonstick pan.*

2.   Prepare pan.   *Grease muffin tin or fill with paper liners. A nonstick baking pan requires no greasing.*

3.   Assemble ingredients.   *Place all ingredients on the counter. Have your ingredients chopped and grated beforehand. If you have a food processor, use it to puree, grate fruits and vegetables, mash bananas, chop dried fruits and herbs. A blender is also useful.*

4.   Assemble utensils.   *Place on your working area: one large bowl, approximately 10-inch (250-mm) diameter; one smaller bowl, approximately 8-inch (200-mm) diameter; a set of measuring cups; a set of measuring spoons; a wire whisk or fork; one spatula; one large spoon.*

5.   Measure wet ingredients.   *Add egg(s) to bowl together with sugar, oil, and liquid. Combine well with whisk or fork; it is not necessary to beat mixture. However, if you*

are doubling the recipe, place wet ingredients in bowl and beat briefly with hand mixer or on low speed of electric mixer. Add fresh fruits or vegetables to wet ingredients and set aside while mixing dry ingredients. If you are adding chopped nuts to the wet ingredients, do so at the last moment, after dry ingredients are added.

6.   Measure dry ingredients.   *Scoop flour lightly into measuring cup and level off with a spatula. Add leaveners and spices and stir well.*

7.   Combine wet and dry ingredients.   *Add dry ingredients all at once to the wet ingredients, and fold together gently. Mix only until the flour is just incorporated. Consistency of batter will vary with recipe, but the texture will be lumpy.*

8.   Spoon batter into muffin pan.   *Tops do not have to be perfectly rounded or uniform. Add topping before baking or place pieces of fruit or nuts on top.*

9.   Bake.   *Place pan on middle rack in one layer for even heat circulation. Test with toothpick to ensure that muffins are fully baked (toothpick should come out dry and clean).*

10.   Remove muffins from pan.   *Let cool slightly in pan, then remove from pan within 10 minutes. Let cool on a wire rack before serving.*

Batter

A proper *batter appears lumpy in the bowl and falls in lumps off the spoon. It produces a baked muffin with an even texture, with no large holes or tunnels. The muffin is moist and tender.*

An overmixed *batter brings out the gluten in the flour, making the dough smooth and elastic. The dough stretches into strands when lifted with a spoon. It produces an uneven texture, with holes and tunnels. The muffin will be tough and dry.*

Flour

All recipes were tested with ordinary all-purpose flour, measured straight from the package. Flour may differ by up to 20 percent in the amount of moisture it will absorb, but these variations will not make an appreciable difference.

Oil

These muffins have been made with sunflower oil. Avoid "vegetable oils" because they are highly variable blends of oils and will not always give successful muffins.

HELPFUL HINTS

♥ *Shiny muffin tins reflect heat, whereas dull ones absorb heat. Dull pans result in a browner crust. If using a dark nonstick pan, reduce the temperature by 25°F (10°C) and fill one cup with water to provide extra moisture.*

♥ *When doubling a recipe, cut back on seasonings such as salt, cinnamon, etc. When a single recipe calls for 1 teaspoon seasoning, adjust to 1½ teaspoons for doubling.*

♥ *If using nonfat dry milk as liquid milk substitute, put dry milk into dry ingredients and add water to equal measure to the wet ingredients.*

♥ *To keep crusts from burning, leave one muffin cup partially filled with water. This also avoids uneven baking.*

♥ *If you have only enough batter to fill half the cups, fill remaining ones with water.*

♥ *Before freezing muffins, allow to cool fully. Wrap in foil or place in airtight plastic containers or bags. Store up to one or two months only.*

♥ *To reheat frozen muffins, cover with foil and place in 400°F (200°C) oven for 25 minutes.*

♥ *To reheat fresh muffins, cover lightly with foil and heat in a 400°F (200°C) oven for 10 minutes, or place in brown paper bag, sprinkle outside with water, and bake at 300°C (150°C) for 20 minutes.*

♥ *Muffins are best eaten within two days of baking. Store in container with loose-fitting top. Muffin tops can become sticky or too moist in an airtight container.*

♥ *Grease pan for savory muffins with leftover bacon fat.*

♥ *To grease a pan quickly, slip hand into a plastic bag, then grease.*

♥ *If you want your muffins with a soft outside, use paper cup liners.*

♥ *If you like extra-large muffins, grease top of muffin pan between the cups.*

♥ *To clean an encrusted pan, soak in cold water sprinkled with baking soda and let stand several hours. Then wash.*

♥ *Use crumbled leftover muffins as toppings for casseroles. This is especially good with leftover savory muffins.*

SWEET MUFFINS

APPLE CARROT

MAKES 12 MEDIUM

*Preheat oven to 375°F (190°C)
and prepare pan.*

IN LARGE BOWL ADD AND COMBINE WELL

3 eggs
⅔ cup (125 g) sugar
½ cup (125 mL) oil
1 cup (125 g) shredded apple
1 cup (140 g) shredded carrots
1 tsp. vanilla

♥

IN SMALLER BOWL COMBINE WELL

1 cup (140 g) graham flour
1 cup (140 g) cake flour
1 Tbsp. baking powder
½ tsp. baking soda
½ tsp. salt
½ tsp. ground cinnamon
½ cup (60 g) chopped walnuts or
pecans (optional)

Combine wet and dry mixtures and fold together gently until just mixed. Spoon into prepared pan and decorate top of each muffin with a walnut or pecan half. Bake at 375°F (190°C) for 25 to 30 minutes. Remove from pan and cool on rack.

Hint

Toss shredded apple in lemon juice to prevent darkening.

Serving Suggestion

Make Cinnamon Crumble Topping—Mix 4 Tbsp. (40 g) sugar, 2 Tbsp. (14 g) flour, ½ tsp. cinnamon, and 1 Tbsp. softened butter. Mix well by rubbing together with fingers. Sprinkle on muffin tops before baking.

Opposite: Apple Carrot Muffins with Cinnamon Crumble Topping

Combine wet and dry mixtures and fold together gently until just mixed. Spoon into prepared pan. Bake at 400°F (200°C) for 20 minutes. Remove from pan and cool on rack.

Hint

The apple flavor is more apparent when eaten cold.

Serving Suggestion

Serve with unsalted butter and cheddar cheese for breakfast or lunch, or with cottage cheese and fruit.

APPLE BRAN

MAKES 8 LARGE OR 12 MEDIUM

Preheat oven to 400°F (200°C) and prepare pan.

IN LARGE BOWL ADD AND COMBINE WELL

2 eggs
¼ cup (60 mL) unsulphured molasses
¼ cup (60 mL) honey
½ cup (125 mL) oil
1 cup (85 g) All-Bran cereal
1½ cups (170 g) lightly packed chopped apples
¼ cup (40 g) raisins

♥

IN SMALLER BOWL COMBINE WELL

1 cup (140 g) all-purpose flour
2 tsp. baking soda
½ tsp. ground cinnamon
¼ tsp. ground nutmeg
¼ cup (30 g) chopped walnuts

APPLE CINNAMON

MAKES 12 MEDIUM

*Preheat oven to 400°F (200°C)
and prepare pan.*

IN LARGE BOWL ADD AND COMBINE WELL

2 eggs
½ cup (85 g) brown sugar
½ cup (125 mL) oil
½ cup (125 mL) apple juice
2 cups (225 g) chopped apples
¼ cup (40 g) raisins
1 tsp. vanilla

♥

IN SMALLER BOWL COMBINE WELL

1 cup (140 g) whole-wheat flour
1 cup (140 g) cake flour
1 Tbsp. baking powder
½ tsp. baking soda
½ tsp. salt
1 tsp. ground cinnamon
½ cup (60 g) chopped walnuts
(optional)

*Combine wet and dry
mixtures and fold together
until just mixed. Spoon into
prepared pan. Bake at 400°F
(200°C) for 20 to 25 minutes.
Remove from pan and cool
on rack.*

Variation

APPLE GINGER *Omit cinnamon
and raisins. Add 8 pieces finely
chopped crystallized ginger (or to
taste) and toss into dry mixture.*

Serving Suggestion

*Make Cinnamon Sugar Topping—Mix
½ cup (80 g) granulated sugar with
1 Tbsp. cinnamon. Melt ¼ cup
(60 g) butter and dip hot muffins in
melted butter, then in cinnamon
sugar. Serve. Store leftover cinnamon
sugar in a covered jar.*

Combine wet and dry mixtures and fold together gently until just mixed. Bake at 400°F (200°C) for 20 to 25 minutes. Remove from pan and cool on rack.

Variation

APPLE WHEAT *Substitute wheat flakes for rolled oats. Wheat flakes are available in natural foods stores.*

Hint

For true oatmeal flavor, use old-fashioned rolled oats. Quick-cooking, not instant, oatmeal may be substituted, but the pleasant chewiness will be lost.

APPLE OATMEAL

MAKES 10 LARGE OR 14 MEDIUM

Preheat oven to 400°F (200°C) and prepare pan.

IN LARGE BOWL ADD AND COMBINE WELL

2 eggs
3 Tbsp. honey
½ cup (125 mL) oil
1 cup (240 mL) milk
1 cup (150 g) rolled oats
2 cups (225 g) chopped apples
½ cup (85 g) raisins
1 tsp. vanilla

IN SMALLER BOWL COMBINE WELL

2 cups (280 g) all-purpose flour
1 Tbsp. baking powder
½ tsp. baking soda
½ tsp. salt
1 tsp. ground cinnamon

APPLE PLUS

MAKES 10 LARGE OR 14 MEDIUM

Preheat oven to 400°F (200°C)
and prepare pan.

IN A LARGE BOWL ADD AND COMBINE WELL

2 eggs
¼ cup (60 mL) honey
¼ cup (60 mL) unsulphured molasses
½ cup (125 mL) oil
¾ cup (175 mL) apple juice
1 cup (115 g) finely chopped apple
½ cup (85 g) currants or raisins

♥

IN SMALLER BOWL COMBINE WELL

1 cup (140 g) all-purpose flour
½ cup (70 g) whole-wheat flour
¼ cup (20 g) raw wheat germ
1 Tbsp. baking powder
1 tsp. baking soda
¼ tsp. salt
¼ tsp. ground nutmeg
½ cup (60 g) chopped walnuts or
pecans

Combine wet and dry mixtures and fold together gently until just mixed. Spoon into prepared pan. Bake at 400°F (200°C) for 25 minutes. Remove from pan and cool on rack.

Hint

Molasses will pour out of a measuring cup easily if you measure oil in the same cup first. Raw (untoasted) wheat germ is available in natural foods stores.

Serving Suggestion

Serve with Cinnamon Topping (see Apple Cinnamon muffin), or make Cinnamon Butter by creaming ½ cup (115 g) unsalted butter together with ¼ cup (40 g) cinnamon sugar and beating until light and fluffy.

Combine wet and dry mixtures and fold together gently until just mixed. Spoon into prepared pan. Bake at 400°F (200°C) for 20 to 25 minutes. Remove from pan and cool on rack.

APPLESAUCE SPICE RAISIN

MAKES 12 MEDIUM

Preheat oven to 400°F (200°C) and prepare pan.

IN LARGE BOWL ADD AND COMBINE WELL

2 eggs
⅓ cup (60 g) brown sugar
½ cup (125 mL) oil
1 cup (240 mL) applesauce
½ cup (85 g) raisins

♥

IN SMALLER BOWL COMBINE WELL

1¾ cup (250 g) all-purpose flour
1 tsp. baking powder
1 tsp. baking soda
¼ tsp. salt
½ tsp. ground cinnamon
½ tsp. ground nutmeg
⅛ tsp. ground allspice

Variation

WHOLE-WHEAT APPLESAUCE
Substitute 1 cup (140 g) unsifted whole-wheat flour plus ¾ cup (100 g) unsifted cake flour for 1¾ cup (250 g) all-purpose flour.

APRICOT

MAKES 10 MEDIUM

*Preheat oven to 400°F (200°C)
and prepare pan.*

IN LARGE BOWL ADD AND COMBINE WELL

2 eggs
½ cup (85 g) brown sugar
¼ cup (60 mL) oil
¾ cup (175 mL) prepared
apricot purée
1 tsp. orange extract

♥

IN SMALLER BOWL COMBINE WELL

1½ cups (210 g) all-purpose flour
1 Tbsp. baking powder
½ tsp. baking soda
½ tsp. salt
½ cup (60 g) chopped walnuts or
pecans (optional)

Make apricot purée first. Bring ¼ lb. (115 g) dried apricots plus ¾ cup (175 mL) water to a boil. Cover and simmer 10 to 15 minutes. Put mixture in a food processor or blender and reduce to a purée. (Don't worry if the purée is not totally smooth.) Set aside.

Combine wet and dry mixtures and fold together gently until just mixed. Spoon into prepared pan and decorate top of each muffin with a piece of dried apricot or nut. Bake at 400°F (200°C) for 20 to 25 minutes. Remove from pan and cool on rack.

Variations

PRUNE *Make a prune purée. Prepare as apricot purée (above) substituting equal quantity of pitted dried prunes. Substitute 1 tsp. vanilla for orange extract.*
APRICOT OR PRUNE GRAHAM
Substitute 1 cup (140 g) unsifted graham flour plus ½ cup (70 g) unsifted cake flour for all-purpose flour. Add ½ cup (125 mL) plain yogurt to wet mixture.

*Combine wet and dry
mixtures and fold together
gently until just mixed.
Spoon into prepared pan.
Bake at 400°F (200°C) for 20
minutes. Remove from pan
and cool on rack.*

Hint

*For very young children omit raisins
and nuts.*

Serving Suggestion

A good muffin for youngsters.

BANANA CARROT

MAKES 12 MEDIUM

*Preheat oven to 400°F (200°C)
and prepare pan.*

IN LARGE BOWL ADD AND COMBINE WELL

2 eggs
½ cup (85 g) brown sugar
½ cup (125 mL) oil
½ cup (125 mL) buttermilk
1 cup (125 g) grated carrot
½ cup (125 mL) mashed banana
1 tsp. vanilla
¼ cup (40 g) raisins (optional)

♥

IN SMALLER BOWL COMBINE WELL

1½ cups (210 g) all-purpose flour
2 tsp. baking powder
1 tsp. baking soda
¼ tsp. salt
½ tsp. ground nutmeg
one pinch ground cloves

BANANA

MAKES 10 MEDIUM

Preheat oven to 375°F (190°C) and prepare pan.

IN LARGE BOWL CREAM WITH ELECTRIC MIXER

½ cup (115 g) butter
½ cup (85 g) sugar

♥

ADD AND COMBINE WELL

1 egg
1 cup (240 mL) mashed bananas
1 tsp. baking soda dissolved
in 1 Tbsp. hot water

♥

IN SMALLER BOWL COMBINE WELL

1½ cups (210 g) all-purpose flour
¼ tsp. salt
1 tsp. ground nutmeg
½ cup (60 g) chopped walnuts
(optional)

Combine wet and dry mixtures and fold together gently until just mixed. Spoon into prepared pan and decorate top of each muffin with a walnut half. Bake at 375°F (190°C) for 20 minutes. Remove from pan and cool on rack.

Variations

BANANA PRUNE *Add 1 cup (115 g) chopped pitted prunes to the batter.*

BANANA CAROB *Reduce sugar to ⅓ cup (60 g) and add ¼ cup (35 g) carob powder to dry mixture. Omit nutmeg and add 1 tsp. vanilla to wet mixture.*

BANANA CHOCOLATE CHIP OR CAROB CHIP *Add ½ cup (60 g) chocolate or carob chips to batter.*

Opposite: Banana Chocolate Chip Muffins

Combine wet and dry mixtures and fold together gently until just mixed. Spoon into prepared pan. Bake at 375°F (190°C) for 20 to 25 minutes. Remove from pan and cool on rack.

BANANA COCONUT

**MAKES 24 MINIATURE
OR 12 MEDIUM**

*Preheat oven to 375°F (190°C)
and prepare pan.*

IN LARGE BOWL ADD AND COMBINE WELL

1 egg
½ cup (85 g) sugar
½ cup (115 g) butter or margarine,
melted
½ cup (125 mL) buttermilk
or plain yogurt
½ cup (125 mL) mashed banana
1 tsp. vanilla
1 cup (115 g) sweetened flaked
or shredded coconut

♥

IN SMALLER BOWL COMBINE WELL

1½ cups (210 g) all-purpose flour
1½ tsp. baking powder
1 tsp. baking soda
¼ tsp. salt
½ tsp. ground nutmeg
one pinch ground cloves

Hint

Do not bake with soft margarine.

Serving Suggestion

*Make in miniature pan and serve
with lemon tea.*

BANANA ORANGE

MAKES 12 MEDIUM

*Preheat oven to 400°F (200°C)
and prepare pan.*

IN A FOOD PROCESSOR OR BLENDER
REDUCE TO A PURÉE

1 whole orange, including skin

♥

IN LARGE BOWL ADD AND COMBINE WELL

2 eggs
½ cup (85 g) brown sugar
½ cup (125 mL) oil
2 small mashed bananas
orange purée as prepared above
½ cup (125 mL) orange juice

♥

IN SMALLER BOWL COMBINE WELL

1½ cups (210 g) all-purpose flour
1 Tbsp. baking powder
½ tsp. baking soda
½ tsp. salt
¼ tsp. ground nutmeg
1 cup (115 g) chopped walnuts
(optional)

*Combine wet and dry
mixtures and fold together
gently until just mixed.
Spoon into prepared pan.
Bake at 400°F (200°C) for 20
to 25 minutes. Remove from
pan and cool on rack.*

Hint

*Orange purée and mashed banana
together should measure 1 cup
(250 mL). To grate orange rind with
a food processor, see* Citrus *muffin.*

Combine wet and dry mixtures and fold together gently until just mixed. Spoon into prepared pan. Bake at 400°F (200°C) for 20 minutes. Remove from pan and cool on rack.

BANANA PEANUT BUTTER

MAKES 10 MEDIUM

Preheat oven to 400°F (200°C) and prepare pan.

IN LARGE BOWL ADD AND COMBINE WELL

2 eggs
½ cup (125 mL) honey
½ cup (125 mL) oil
1 cup (240 mL) mashed bananas
½ cup (125 mL) smooth or crunchy peanut butter
1 tsp. vanilla

♥

IN SMALLER BOWL COMBINE WELL

1½ cups (210 g) all-purpose flour
1 Tbsp. baking powder
½ tsp. baking soda
½ tsp. salt

Hint

Make with creamy peanut butter for infants and youngsters.

BLUEBERRY BRAN WHEAT GERM

MAKES 12 LARGE OR 16 MEDIUM

*Preheat oven to 400°F (200°C)
and prepare pan.*

IN LARGE BOWL ADD AND COMBINE WELL

3 eggs
1 cup (190 g) brown sugar
½ cup (125 mL) oil
2 cups (425 mL) buttermilk
1 tsp. vanilla
1 cup (85 g) raw wheat germ
1 cup (60 g) bran

♥

IN SMALLER BOWL COMBINE WELL

2 cups (280 g) all-purpose flour
2 tsp. baking powder
2 tsp. baking soda
½ tsp. salt
1½ cups (250 g) whole fresh or
frozen blueberries

Combine wet and dry mixtures and fold together gently until just mixed. Bake at 400°F (200°C) for 20 to 25 minutes. Remove from pan and cool on rack.

Variation

CRANBERRY BRAN WHEAT GERM
Substitute 1½ cups (250 g) chopped fresh or frozen cranberries for blueberries.

Hint

Do not defrost frozen blueberries or cranberries before using. Defrosted berries produce a highly discolored batter. Raw (untoasted) wheat germ is available in natural foods stores.

Combine wet and dry mixtures and fold together gently until just mixed. Spoon into prepared pans. Bake at 400°F (200°C) for 20 to 25 minutes. Remove from pans and cool on rack.

Variations

BUTTERMILK BRAN WHEAT FLAKE
Substitute 2¹/₂ cups (150 g) bran plus 2 cups (115 g) wheat flakes for 4¹/₂ cups (225 g) bran.
BUTTERMILK BRAN WHEAT GERM
Substitute 2¹/₂ cups (150 g) bran and 2 cups (175 g) wheat germ for 4¹/₂ cups (225 g) bran.
BUTTERMILK BRAN OATMEAL
Substitute 2¹/₂ cups (150 g) bran and 2 cups (225 g) old-fashioned rolled oats for 4¹/₂ cups (225 g) bran.

BUTTERMILK BRAN

MAKES 36 MEDIUM
Preheat oven to 400°F (200°C) and prepare pans.

IN LARGE BOWL ADD AND COMBINE WELL

6 eggs
1 cup (190 g) brown sugar
¹/₂ cup (125 mL) unsulphured molasses
1¹/₂ cups (350 mL) oil
2 tsp. vanilla
1 quart (950 mL) buttermilk
4¹/₂ cups (255 g) bran
1 cup (175 g) chopped prunes or dates
1 cup (175 g) currants or raisins

♥

IN SMALLER BOWL COMBINE WELL

2 cups (280 g) all-purpose flour
2 cups (280 g) whole-wheat flour
4 tsp. baking powder
4 tsp. baking soda
1 cup (115 g) chopped walnuts or pecans (optional)

Combine wet and dry
mixtures and fold together
gently until just mixed.
Spoon into prepared pan.
Bake at 400°F (200°C) for 20
minutes. Remove from pan
and cool on rack.

BUTTERMILK OATMEAL

MAKES 12 MEDIUM

*Preheat oven to 400°F (200°C)
and prepare pan.*

MIX AND ALLOW TO SOAK FOR 10 MINUTES

1½ cups (175 g) old-fashioned
rolled oats
1½ cups (350 mL) buttermilk

♥

IN LARGE BOWL ADD AND COMBINE WELL

2 eggs
½ cup (85 g) brown sugar
½ cup (115 g) butter or margarine,
melted
Rolled oats mixture as prepared
above
1 tsp. vanilla

♥

IN SMALLER BOWL COMBINE WELL

1½ cups (210 g) all-purpose flour
1 Tbsp. baking powder
½ tsp. baking soda
½ tsp. salt
⅛ tsp. ground nutmeg

Variations

OATMEAL BLUEBERRY   *Alter rolled
oats mixture to measure 1 cup
(115 g) rolled oats soaked in 1 cup
(240 mL) buttermilk. Substitute
½ cup (125 mL) graham flour plus
1 cup (140 g) all-purpose flour for
1½ cups (210 g) all-purpose flour.
Add 1 cup (115 g) fresh or frozen
blueberries at the last moment.*
OATMEAL CRANBERRY   *Alter rolled
oats mixture to measure 1 cup
(115 g) rolled oats soaked in 1 cup
(240 mL) buttermilk. Increase brown
sugar to ⅔ cup (125 g). Add 1 cup
(115 g) chopped fresh or frozen
cranberries at the last moment.*

To prepare butternut squash purée, bake one butternut squash (1 lb. or 450 g) until very soft (approx. one hour). Sieve pulp, measure and reserve ¾ cup (175 mL). If you have a blender or food processor, remove seeds and purée pulp.

Combine wet and dry mixtures and fold together gently until just mixed. Spoon into prepared pan and decorate top of each muffin with a walnut or pecan half. Bake at 400°F (200°C) for 20 to 25 minutes. Remove from pan and cool on rack.

Hint

2 cup (60 g) roasted seeds or
ts (pumpkin, sesame or peanuts,
1 nuts, etc.) into batter and
kle additional seeds or nuts on
muffin top.

1 butternut squash may be
ted with good results.

BUTTERNUT SQUASH

MAKES 12 MEDIUM

Preheat oven to 400°F (200°C) and prepare pan.

IN LARGE BOWL ADD AND COMBINE WELL

2 eggs
½ cup (85 g) brown sugar
½ cup (115 g) butter or margarine, melted
¾ cup (175 mL) milk
¾ cup (175 mL) butternut squash purée, prepared as above
½ cup (85 g) raisins

♥

IN SMALLER BOWL COMBINE WELL

1 cup (140 g) all-purpose flour
½ cup (70 g) whole-wheat flour
½ cup (70 g) cake flour
1 Tbsp. baking powder
½ tsp. baking soda
½ tsp. salt
½ tsp. ground cinnamon
½ tsp. ground nutmeg
½ cup chopped walnuts or pecans

CAROB ORANGE

MAKES 14 MEDIUM

*Preheat oven to 400°F (200°C)
and prepare pan.*

IN A FOOD PROCESSOR OR BLENDER
REDUCE TO A PURÉE

1 whole orange, including skin

IN LARGE BOWL ADD AND COMBINE WELL

2 eggs
¼ cup (40 g) brown sugar
¼ cup (60 mL) honey
orange purée as prepared above
½ cup (125 mL) oil
1 cup (240 mL) milk
1 tsp. vanilla

♥

IN SMALLER BOWL COMBINE WELL

2 cups (280 g) all-purpose flour
¼ cup (35 g) carob powder
1 Tbsp. baking powder
½ tsp. baking soda
¼ tsp. ground ginger
½ cup (60 g) chopped walnuts
or pecans

*Combine wet and dry
mixtures and fold together
gently until just mixed.
Spoon into prepared pan.
Bake at 400°F (200°C) for 20
minutes. Remove from pan
and cool on rack.*

Variations

CHOCOLATE ORANGE *Increase
brown sugar to ½ cup (85 g).
Substitute cocoa for carob powder.*
CAROB CHIP *Omit puréed orange.
Substitute ½ cup (60 g) carob chips
for nuts.*

Serving Suggestion

Serve with whipped cream cheese.

Opposite: Blueberry Bran Wheat Germ Muffins
(p. 28)

Combine wet and dry mixtures and fold together gently until just mixed. Spoon into prepared pan. Bake at 400°F (200°C) for 20 minutes. Remove from pan and cool on rack.

Variations

BACON CHEDDAR   *Omit salt. Add ½ cup (60 g) fried, crisp, crumbled bacon to batter when combining wet and dry mixtures.*

APPLE CHEDDAR   *Makes 12 medium. Omit prepared mustard. Add 1 cup (115 g) peeled chopped apple to wet mixture.*

DATE CHEESE   *Makes 12 medium. Omit prepared mustard. Add ¾ cup (125 g) chopped dates to wet mixture.*

BUTTERY CARROT   *Makes 12 medium. Substitute ¾ cup (85 g) mild cheddar (not medium) for sharp cheese. Add 1 cup (115 g) grated carrot to wet mixture. Substitute 1½ cups (210 g) all-purpose flour for whole-wheat/cake flour mixture.*

CHEDDAR

MAKES 10 MEDIUM

Preheat oven to 400°F (200°C) and prepare pan.

IN LARGE BOWL ADD AND COMBINE WELL

2 eggs
¼ cup (60 mL) honey or maple syrup
¼ cup (60 mL) oil
½ cup (125 mL) buttermilk
or plain yogurt
1 cup (115 g) grated sharp
cheddar cheese
1 tsp. prepared mustard

♥

IN SMALLER BOWL COMBINE WELL

1 cup (140 g) cake flour
½ cup (70 g) whole-wheat flour
1½ tsp. baking powder
½ tsp. baking soda
½ tsp. salt

Combine wet and dry mixtures and fold together gently until just mixed. Spoon into prepared pan. Bake at 400°F (200°C) for 20 minutes. Remove from pan and cool on rack.

CHERRY ALMOND OR PECAN

MAKES 12 MEDIUM

Preheat oven to 400°F (200°C) and prepare pan.

IN LARGE BOWL ADD AND COMBINE WELL

4 eggs
½ cup (85 g) sugar
½ cup (115 g) butter or margarine, melted
1 cup (225 g) whole pitted sour cherries (1 14-oz. or 398-mL can, drained)
½ tsp. almond extract

♥

IN SMALLER BOWL COMBINE WELL

2 cups (280 g) all-purpose flour
1 Tbsp. baking powder
1 tsp. baking soda
¼ tsp. salt
1 cup (115 g) finely chopped almonds or pecans

Variations

FRUIT COCKTAIL *Substitute 1 cup (225 g) well-drained fruit cocktail (1 14-oz. or 398-mL can) for sour red cherries. Omit nuts.*

Hint

The Cherry Almond or Pecan muffin looks and tastes its best when canned pitted cherries are left whole and nuts are finely chopped.

Serving Suggestion

Make the Fruit Cocktail muffin for children and decorate the top of each muffin with a maraschino cherry half.

Combine wet and dry mixtures and fold together gently until just mixed. Spoon into prepared pan and decorate top with a maraschino cherry half. Bake at 400°F (200°C) for 15 to 20 minutes. Remove from pan and cool on rack.

Hint

Maraschino cherries, as well as candied or dried fruits, are chopped easily with kitchen shears.

Serving Suggestion

A pretty muffin that needs no butter. Make in miniature pan for a party or tea-time sweet. Decorate the top of each muffin with a maraschino cherry half.

CHERRY PINEAPPLE

MAKES 24 MINIATURE OR 12 MEDIUM

Preheat oven to 400°F (200°C) and prepare pan.

IN LARGE BOWL ADD AND COMBINE WELL

2 eggs
⅓ cup (60 g) sugar
¼ cup (60 g) butter or margarine, melted
¼ cup (60 mL) maraschino cherry juice
1 cup (240 mL) unsweetened crushed pineapple, with juice
¼ cup (40 g) coarsely chopped maraschino cherries
½ tsp. almond extract

♥

IN SMALLER BOWL COMBINE WELL

2 cups (280 g) all-purpose flour
1 Tbsp. baking powder
½ tsp. baking soda
½ tsp. salt

CHOCOLATE CHOCOLATE CHIP

MAKES 10 MEDIUM

*Preheat oven to 400°F (200°C)
and prepare pan.*

IN LARGE BOWL ADD AND COMBINE WELL

2 eggs
½ cup (125 mL) oil
1 cup (240 mL) milk
1 tsp. vanilla

♥

IN SMALLER BOWL COMBINE WELL

1¾ cups (240 g) all-purpose flour
½ cup (85 g) sugar
¼ cup (35 g) cocoa
1 Tbsp. baking powder
½ tsp. salt
½ cup (85 g) semi-sweet
chocolate chips

*Combine wet and dry
mixtures and fold together
gently until just mixed.
Spoon into prepared pan.
Bake at 400°F (200°C) for 20
minutes. Remove from pan
and cool on rack.*

Variations

MAPLE BUTTERSCOTCH CHIP
*Substitute light brown sugar for
granulated. Omit cocoa and adjust
all-purpose flour to 2 cups (240 g).
Substitute 1 tsp. maple extract for
vanilla and butterscotch chips for
chocolate chips.*
**CHOCOLATE PEANUT BUTTER
CHIP** *Substitute peanut butter chips
for chocolate chips.*

Hint

*Sprinkle extra chocolate chips on top
of each muffin before baking.*

Combine wet and dry mixtures and fold together gently until just mixed. Spoon into prepared pan. Bake at 400°F (200°C) for 20 minutes. Remove from pan and cool on rack.

Hint

To grate citrus peel with a food processor, remove the peel, chop into 1" pieces and process together with ¼ cup (40 g) or ½ cup (85 g) of sugar. Calculate sugar into the recipe. Try not to remove any of the bitter white membrane underneath the peel. If the fruit is thick skinned and firm, peel can be removed easily with a vegetable peeler.

CITRUS (LEMON ORANGE)

MAKES 24 MINIATURE OR 12 MEDIUM

Preheat oven to 400°F (200°C) and prepare pan.

IN LARGE BOWL ADD AND COMBINE WELL

2 eggs
½ cup (85 g) sugar
½ cup (125 mL) oil
½ cup (125 mL) milk
grated rind of 1 lemon
grated rind of 1 orange
juice of 1 lemon
juice of 1 orange
(lemon and orange juice should measure ½ cup (125 mL) together)

♥

IN SMALLER BOWL COMBINE WELL

1¼ cups (175 g) cake flour
1 cup (140 g) whole-wheat flour
1 Tbsp. baking powder
½ tsp. baking soda
½ tsp. salt

CITRUS ZUCCHINI/ COURGETTE

MAKES 24 MINIATURE OR 12 MEDIUM

Preheat oven to 400°F (200°C) and prepare pan.

IN LARGE BOWL ADD AND COMBINE WELL

2 eggs
⅔ cup (125 g) sugar
½ cup (125 mL) oil
grated rind of 1 lemon
juice of 1 lemon
1½ cups (210 g) unpeeled, grated
zucchini/courgettes

♥

IN SMALLER BOWL COMBINE WELL

2 cups (280 g) all-purpose flour
2 tsp. baking powder
½ tsp. baking soda
¼ tsp. salt
⅛ tsp. ground nutmeg

Combine wet and dry mixtures and fold together gently until just mixed. Spoon into prepared pan. Bake at 400°F (200°C) for 20 to 25 minutes. Remove from pan and cool on rack.

Serving Suggestion

Make miniatures, hollow out slightly and fill with lemon curd. Serve larger muffins with Lemon Cream Cheese Spread. *First make* Lemon Butter *(see* Cranberry Nut *muffin) and mix equal quantities of cream cheese and* Lemon Butter *and beat until light and fluffy.*

Combine wet and dry mixtures and fold together gently until just mixed. Spoon into prepared pan. Bake at 400°F (200°C) for 20 to 25 minutes. Remove from pan and cool on rack.

Variations

CHOCOLATE COCONUT *Add 3 Tbsp. (25 g) cocoa plus an additional ¹/₄ cup (40 g) sugar to dry mixture.*
CAROB COCONUT *Add 3 Tbsp. (25 g) carob powder to dry mixture.*
CHOCOLATE CHIP COCONUT *Add ¹/₂ cup (85 g) semi-sweet chocolate chips to coconut or chocolate coconut muffin batter.*

COCONUT

**MAKES 26 MINIATURE
OR 14 MEDIUM**

*Preheat oven to 400°F (200°C)
and prepare pan.*

IN LARGE BOWL ADD AND COMBINE WELL

2 eggs
½ cup (85 g) sugar
½ cup (115 g) butter or
margarine, melted
¾ cup (175 mL) milk
2 tsp. grated lemon rind
1½ cups (175 g) flaked sweetened
coconut

♥

IN SMALLER BOWL COMBINE WELL

1½ cups (210 g) cake flour
1½ tsp. baking powder
½ tsp. baking soda
¼ tsp. salt

CRANBERRY NUT

MAKES 12 MEDIUM

*Preheat oven to 400°F (200°C)
and prepare pan.*

IN LARGE BOWL ADD AND COMBINE WELL

2 eggs
¼ cup (60 g) butter or
margarine, melted
1 cup (240 mL) milk
1 tsp. vanilla

♥

IN SMALLER BOWL COMBINE WELL

2 cups (280 g) all-purpose flour
¾ cup (150 g) sugar
1 Tbsp. baking powder
½ tsp. baking soda
½ tsp. salt
1½ cups (350 g) chopped fresh
or frozen cranberries
½ cup (60 g) chopped walnuts
(optional)

*Combine wet and dry
mixtures and fold together
gently until just mixed.
Spoon into prepared pan.
Bake at 400°F (200°C) for 25
minutes. Remove from pan
and cool on rack.*

Variation

BLUEBERRY NUT   *Substitute whole
fresh or frozen blueberries for
cranberries. Substitute 1 tsp. grated
lemon rind for vanilla.*

Hint

*Do not defrost frozen blueberries or
cranberries before using. Defrosted
berries produce a highly discolored
batter.*

Serving Suggestion

Blueberry Nut *goes especially well
with* Lemon Butter. *Make* Lemon
Butter—*Grate the rind of 3 lemons
(approx. 3 Tbsp.) and mix well with
½ cup (85 g) granulated sugar. Add
to 1 cup (250 mL) unsalted butter
and beat until light and fluffy.*

Opposite: Cranberry Nut Muffins

Combine wet and dry mixtures and fold together gently until just mixed. Spoon into prepared pan. Bake at 400°F (200°C) for 20 minutes. Remove from pan and cool on rack.

Variation

CORNMEAL WITH PRESERVES
Spoon 1 tsp. preserves on top of each muffin before baking (see Peach Puffins*).*

Hint

Raw (untoasted) wheat germ is available in natural foods stores.

CORN
WHEAT GERM

MAKES 15 MEDIUM OR 12 LARGE

Preheat oven to 400°F (200°C) and prepare pan.

MIX AND ALLOW TO SOAK FOR 10 MINUTES

1 cup (190 g) cornmeal
2 cups (425 mL) buttermilk

♥

IN LARGE BOWL ADD AND COMBINE WELL

2 eggs
½ cup (85 g) sugar
½ cup (125 mL) oil
Cornmeal mixture as prepared above

♥

IN SMALLER BOWL COMBINE WELL

1¾ cups (250 g) all-purpose flour
1 cup (85 g) wheat germ
2 tsp. baking powder
1 tsp. baking soda
1 tsp. salt

CREAM OF WHEAT

MAKES 12 MEDIUM

Preheat oven to 400°F (200°C) and prepare pan.

IN LARGE BOWL ADD AND COMBINE WELL

2 eggs
½ cup (115 g) butter or
margarine, melted
1 cup (240 mL) milk
1 tsp. vanilla

♥

IN SMALLER BOWL COMBINE WELL

1¼ cups (175 g) all-purpose flour
¾ cup (125 g) cream of wheat
½ cup (85 g) sugar
1 Tbsp. baking powder
½ tsp. salt

Combine wet and dry mixtures and fold together gently until just mixed. Spoon into prepared pan. Bake at 400°F (200°C) for 20 minutes. Remove from pan and cool on rack.

Variation

DURUM SEMOLINA OR FARINA
Substitute semolina or farina for cream of wheat.

Serving Suggestions

For young children, place 1 tsp. jam on top of each muffin. With the back of a spoon, gently press half of the jam into the muffin. Bake and cool well. Do not use jelly; it will melt and run onto the pan.

This muffin is also good with an Apple-Cinnamon topping (see Rice muffin).

Combine wet and dry mixtures and fold together gently until just mixed. Spoon into prepared pan and sprinkle top of each muffin with chopped peanuts. Bake at 375°F (190°C) for 25 minutes. Remove from pan and cool on rack.

Variation

Omit salt and substitute ½ cup (85 g) roasted pumpkin seeds for chopped peanuts. Sprinkle additional pumpkin seeds on each muffin top before baking.

Hint

To liquify honey that has crystallized, place honey pot or jar in hot water. Do not bake with hardened creamed honey. Freshly ground peanut butter is often sold in supermarkets and natural foods stores.

CRUNCHY PEANUT BUTTER AND HONEY

MAKES 14 MEDIUM

Preheat oven to 375°F (190°C) and prepare pan.

IN LARGE BOWL ADD AND COMBINE WELL

2 eggs
½ cup (125 mL) honey
¼ cup (60 mL) oil
1 cup (240 mL) buttermilk
1 cup (240 mL) freshly ground peanut butter
1 tsp. vanilla

♥

IN SMALLER BOWL COMBINE WELL

1 cup (140 g) whole-wheat flour
1 cup (140 g) cake flour
2 tsp. baking powder
1 tsp. baking soda
½ tsp. salt
½ cup (60 g) unsalted chopped peanuts

FLAXSEED

MAKES 12 MEDIUM

*Preheat oven to 400°F (200°C)
and prepare pan.*

IN LARGE BOWL ADD AND COMBINE WELL

2 eggs
¼ cup (60 mL) honey
¼ cup (40 g) brown sugar
½ cup (125 mL) oil
1 cup (240 mL) buttermilk
1 tsp. vanilla

♥

IN SMALLER BOWL COMBINE WELL

1 cup (140 g) all-purpose flour
1 cup (115 g) ground flaxseed
1 tsp. baking powder
1 tsp. baking soda
¼ tsp. salt
1 tsp. ground cinnamon
½ cup (60 g) chopped walnuts
or pecans

*Combine wet and dry
mixtures and fold together
gently until just mixed.
Spoon into prepared pan
and decorate top of each
muffin with a walnut or
pecan half. Bake at 400°F
(200°C) for 20 minutes.
Remove from pan and cool
on rack.*

Hint

*An effective alternative to bran or
prune. Grind flaxseeds in a coffee
grinder if a nut grinder is not
available.*

Combine wet and dry mixtures and fold together gently until just mixed. Spoon into prepared pan. Bake at 375°F (190°C) for 15 to 20 minutes. Remove from pan and cool on rack.

Hint

When chopping dried fruit, avoid stickiness by tossing fruit in a small amount of flour first, then calculate the flour into your recipe. If you have a food processor, add the dried fruit plus ¼ or ½ cup flour (40 to 85 g) to processor bowl and chop. Raw (untoasted) wheat germ is available in natural foods stores.

FLOURLESS BRAN

MAKES 8 MEDIUM

Preheat oven to 375°F (190°C) and prepare pan.

IN LARGE BOWL ADD AND COMBINE WELL

2 eggs
2 Tbsp. honey
2 Tbsp. unsulphured molasses
¼ cup (60 mL) oil
1 cup (240 mL) buttermilk
½ cup (85 g) chopped dates
or raisins

♥

IN SMALLER BOWL COMBINE WELL

1½ cups (85 g) bran
1 cup (85 g) raw wheat germ
1½ tsp. baking powder
1 tsp. baking soda
½ cup (60 g) chopped walnuts or
pecans or sunflower seeds

GINGER NUT

MAKES 12 MEDIUM

*Preheat oven to 400°F (200°C)
and prepare pan.*

IN LARGE BOWL ADD AND COMBINE WELL

2 eggs
½ cup (85 g) brown sugar
½ cup (125 mL) oil
1 cup (240 mL) plain yogurt
or buttermilk

♥

IN SMALLER BOWL COMBINE WELL

1 cup (140 g) whole-wheat flour
1 cup (140 g) cake flour
8 pieces finely chopped
crystallized ginger
1 tsp. baking powder
1 tsp. baking soda
½ cup (60 g) chopped pecans
or walnuts

*Combine wet and dry
mixtures and fold together
gently until just mixed.
Spoon into prepared pan
and decorate top of each
muffin with a walnut or
pecan half. Bake at 400°F
(200°C) for 20 to 25 minutes.
Remove from pan and cool
on rack.*

Variation

CHOCOLATE GINGER NUT
*Substitute 2 cups (280 g) all-purpose
flour for whole-wheat and cake flour.
In blender or food processor, chop ½
cup (85 g) semi-sweet chocolate chips
into smaller chips and add to dry
mixture.*

Combine wet and dry mixtures and fold together gently until just mixed. Spoon into prepared pan and sprinkle each muffin top with granola. Bake at 400°F (200°C) for 15 to 20 minutes. Remove from pan and cool on rack.

Hint

Best results are achieved when the granola is not overly sweet and separates easily.

GRANOLA

MAKES 10 LARGE OR 14 MEDIUM

Preheat oven to 400°F (200°C) and prepare pan.

IN LARGE BOWL ADD AND COMBINE WELL

2 eggs
¼ cup (40 g) brown sugar
½ cup (125 mL) oil
1 cup (240 mL) buttermilk
1 tsp. vanilla

♥

IN SMALLER BOWL COMBINE WELL

2 cups (225 g) granola
1 cup (140 g) all-purpose flour
2 tsp. baking powder
½ tsp. baking soda
½ tsp. salt

JAM PUFFINS

MAKES 12 MEDIUM

*Preheat oven to 400°F (200°C)
and prepare pan.*

IN LARGE BOWL ADD AND COMBINE WELL

2 eggs
½ cup (85 g) brown sugar
½ cup (115 g) butter or
margarine, melted
1¼ cups (300 mL) buttermilk
1 tsp. maple extract

♥

IN SMALLER BOWL COMBINE WELL

1 cup (140 g) whole-wheat flour
1 cup (140 g) cake flour
1 tsp. baking powder
1 tsp. baking soda
½ tsp. salt

♥

TOPPING

12 tsp. (60 mL) peach jam

*Combine wet and dry
mixtures and fold together
gently until just mixed.
Spoon into prepared pan (fill
only ⅔ full). Place 1 tsp.
peach jam on each muffin
top and press jam gently with
spoon. Bake at 400°F (200°C)
for 20 minutes. Remove from
pan and cool on rack.*

Variation

RED JAM PUFFINS *Substitute
strawberry or raspberry jam for peach
jam. Substitute 1 tsp. vanilla for
maple extract.*

Opposite: Jam Puffins

Combine wet and dry mixtures and fold together gently until just mixed. Spoon into prepared pan and decorate top of each muffin with a pecan half. Bake at 400°F (200°C) for 20 minutes. Remove from pan and cool on rack.

Variation

MAPLE WALNUT *Substitute 1 cup (115 g) chopped walnuts for ¹/₂ cup (60 g) chopped pecans.*

Serving Suggestion

Good warm with marmalade or Cinnamon Butter *(see* Apple Plus *muffin).*

MAPLE GRAHAM

MAKES 10 MEDIUM

Preheat oven to 400°F (200°C) and prepare pan.

IN LARGE BOWL ADD AND COMBINE WELL

2 eggs
½ cup (125 mL) maple syrup
½ cup (125 mL) oil
¾ cup (175 mL) buttermilk
½ tsp. maple extract

♥

IN SMALLER BOWL COMBINE WELL

1 cup (140 g) graham flour
½ cup (70 g) cake flour
1½ tsp. baking powder
½ tsp. baking soda
½ tsp. salt
½ cup (60 g) chopped pecans

MOCHA ALMOND

MAKES 20 MINIATURE OR 10 MEDIUM

Preheat oven to 400°F (200°C) and prepare pan.

IN LARGE BOWL ADD AND COMBINE WELL

2 tsp. instant coffee dissolved in
1 Tbsp. hot water
1 egg
¼ cup (60 mL) oil
1 cup (240 mL) milk
1 tsp. orange or vanilla extract

♥

IN SMALLER BOWL COMBINE WELL

1½ cups (210 g) all-purpose flour
½ cup (85 g) sugar
2 Tbsp. cocoa
1 tsp. baking powder
½ tsp. baking soda
¼ tsp. salt
½ cup (60 g) chopped or sliced
almonds

Combine wet and dry mixtures and fold together gently until just mixed. Spoon into prepared pan and decorate top of each muffin with chopped or sliced almonds. Bake at 400°F (200°C) for 25 minutes. Remove from pan and cool on rack.

Serving Suggestion

Make in miniature and serve after dinner with coffee.

Combine wet and dry mixtures and fold together gently until just mixed. Spoon into prepared pan. Bake at 400°F (200°C) for 20 to 25 minutes. Remove from pan and cool on rack.

Hint

Sweetened flaked or shredded coconut may be substituted, but decrease sugar to ¹/₂ cup (85 g) and increase all-purpose flour to 1¹/₄ cups (175 g). Raw (untoasted) wheat germ is available in natural foods stores.

OATMEAL COCONUT

MAKES 14 MEDIUM

Preheat oven to 400°F (200°C) and prepare pan.

COMBINE AND ALLOW TO COOL

1 cup (115 g) old-fashioned rolled oats
1 cup (240 mL) boiling water
½ cup (115 g) butter or margarine

♥

IN LARGE BOWL ADD AND COMBINE WELL

2 eggs
¾ cup (150 g) brown sugar
oats mixture as prepared above
1 tsp. vanilla

♥

IN SMALLER BOWL COMBINE WELL

1 cup (140 g) all-purpose flour
½ cup (40 g) raw wheat germ
1 cup (115 g) unsweetened shredded coconut
1 Tbsp. baking powder
½ tsp. baking soda
½ tsp. salt

OATMEAL PINEAPPLE

MAKES 12 MEDIUM

*Preheat oven to 400°F (200°C)
and prepare pan.*

IN LARGE BOWL ADD AND COMBINE WELL

2 eggs
½ cup (85 g) brown sugar
½ cup (125 mL) oil
¼ cup (50 mL) milk or orange juice
1 cup (240 mL) unsweetened crushed
pineapple, with juice
1 cup (115 g) old-fashioned
rolled oats
1 tsp. grated orange rind

♥

IN SMALLER BOWL COMBINE WELL

1½ cups (210 g) all-purpose flour
1 Tbsp. baking powder
½ tsp. baking soda
½ tsp. salt

*Combine wet and dry
mixtures and fold together
gently until just mixed.
Spoon into prepared pan.
Bake at 400°F (200°C) for 20
to 25 minutes. Remove from
pan and cool on rack.*

Variation

OATMEAL APPLE   *Substitute 1 cup
(115 g) grated apple for crushed
pineapple. Add ½ cup (85 g) raisins.*

Hint

*This muffin is best when fully cooled.
Freezes well.*

Combine wet and dry mixtures and fold together gently until just mixed. Spoon into prepared pan. Bake at 400°F (200°C) for 15 minutes. Remove from pan and cool on rack.

Variation

OATMEAL FIG *Substitute ½ cup (85 g) chopped dried dark figs for prunes. Add ½ cup (60 g) chopped walnuts or pecans.*

Hint

This batter is stark white and very thick. The baked muffin is very light in color.

OATMEAL PRUNE

MAKES 12 LARGE OR 15 MEDIUM

Preheat oven to 400°F (200°C) and prepare pan.

IN LARGE BOWL ADD AND COMBINE WELL

2 eggs
¼ cup (60 mL) oil
1 cup (240 mL) milk
1 tsp. vanilla
1 cup (175 g) chopped pitted prunes

♥

IN SMALLER BOWL COMBINE WELL

2 cups (280 g) cake flour
1 cup (115 g) old-fashioned rolled oats
¾ cup (150 g) sugar
1 Tbsp. baking powder
¾ tsp. salt

ORANGE

MAKES 12 MEDIUM

*Preheat oven to 400°F (200°C)
and prepare pan.*

IN A FOOD PROCESSOR OR BLENDER
REDUCE TO A PURÉE

1 whole orange, including skin

♥

IN LARGE BOWL AND COMBINE WELL

1 egg
½ cup (85 g) brown sugar
orange purée as prepared above
½ cup (125 mL) oil
½ cup (125 mL) orange juice
¼ cup (85 g) chopped dark figs
¼ cup (40 g) chopped dates

♥

IN SMALLER BOWL COMBINE WELL

½ cup (70 g) all-purpose flour
½ cup (40 g) wheat germ
½ cup (30 g) bran
1 tsp. baking powder
1 tsp. baking soda
¼ tsp. salt

*Combine wet and dry
mixtures and fold together
gently until just mixed.
Spoon into prepared pan.
Bake at 400°F (200°C) for 15
to 20 minutes. Remove from
pan and cool on rack.*

Spoon into prepared pan. Bake at 375°F (190°C) for 20 to 25 minutes. Remove from pan and cool on rack.

ORANGE FRENCH BREAKFAST

MAKES 8 MEDIUM

Preheat oven to 375°F (190°C) and prepare pan.

IN LARGE BOWL CREAM WITH ELECTRIC MIXER

¼ cup (60 g) shortening
2 Tbsp. (30 g) butter
½ cup (85 g) sugar
2 eggs
grated rind of 1 orange

♥

IN SMALLER BOWL COMBINE WELL

1½ cups (210 g) cake flour
1½ tsp. baking powder
½ tsp. baking soda
½ tsp. salt
¼ tsp. ground nutmeg

♥

ADD FLOUR MIXTURE TO CREAMED MIXTURE ALTERNATELY WITH

½ cup (125 mL) milk

Variation

PLAIN FRENCH BREAKFAST   *Omit grated orange rind and substitute ½ tsp. vanilla extract.*

Serving Suggestions

Citrus marmalade goes well with either, but Plain French Breakfast *is especially tasty with* Cinnamon Sugar Topping *(see* Apple Cinnamon muffin).

PEANUT BUTTER BRAN

MAKES 10 MEDIUM

Preheat oven to 400°F (200°C) and prepare pan.

IN LARGE BOWL CREAM WITH
ELECTRIC MIXER

1 egg
½ cup (85 g) brown sugar
¼ cup (60 g) butter
½ cup (125 mL) peanut butter,
smooth or crunchy

♥

THEN ADD

1 cup (85 g) All-Bran cereal
1 cup (240 mL) milk

♥

IN SMALLER BOWL COMBINE WELL

1 cup (140 g) all-purpose flour
1 Tbsp. baking powder
¼ tsp. baking soda
½ tsp. salt

Combine wet and dry mixtures and fold together gently until just mixed. Spoon into prepared pan. Bake at 400°F (200°C) for 20 to 25 minutes. Remove from pan and cool on rack.

Hint

When made with creamy peanut butter, a good muffin for an infant.

Combine wet and dry mixtures and fold together gently until just mixed. Spoon into prepared pan and decorate top of each muffin with a nut half or apricot piece. Bake at 375°F (190°C) for 25 to 30 minutes. Remove from pan and cool on rack.

Variations

PINEAPPLE APRICOT COCONUT
Substitute ½ cup (60 g) flaked or shredded coconut for nuts.
PINEAPPLE CARROT *Substitute 1 cup (150 g) grated carrots for dried apricots. Add ¼ tsp. ground allspice to dry mixture.*
PINEAPPLE CARROT ORANGE
Substitute grated rind of 1 orange (approx. 1½ Tbsp.) for the lemon in Pineapple Carrot.

PINEAPPLE APRICOT NUT

MAKES 15 MEDIUM
Preheat oven to 375°F (190°C) and prepare pan.

IN LARGE BOWL ADD AND COMBINE WELL
4 eggs
¾ cup (150 g) sugar
1 cup (240 mL) oil
1 cup (240 mL) unsweetened crushed pineapple, with juice
¾ cup (125 g) finely chopped dried apricots
grated rind of 1 lemon

♥

IN SMALLER BOWL COMBINE WELL
2 cups (280 g) all-purpose flour
1 Tbsp. baking powder
½ tsp. baking soda
½ tsp. salt
½ cup (60 g) chopped almonds, pecans, or walnuts

PINEAPPLE COTTAGE CHEESE

MAKES 12 MEDIUM

*Preheat oven to 400°F (200°C)
and prepare pan.*

IN LARGE BOWL ADD AND COMBINE WELL

4 eggs
⅓ cup (60 g) brown sugar
½ cup (125 mL) oil
1 cup (240 mL) cream-style
cottage cheese
1 cup (240 mL) crushed pineapple,
with juice
1 tsp. vanilla

♥

IN SMALLER BOWL COMBINE WELL

1 cup (140 g) whole-wheat flour
1 cup (140 g) cake flour
1 Tbsp. baking powder
½ tsp. baking soda
¼ tsp. salt
¼ tsp. nutmeg

*Combine wet and dry
mixtures and fold together
gently until just mixed.
Spoon into prepared pan.
Bake at 400°F (200°C) for 20
minutes. Remove from pan
and cool on rack.*

Variation

**FRUIT COCKTAIL COTTAGE
CHEESE** *Substitute 1 cup (240 mL)
well-drained fruit cocktail (1 14-oz.
or 398-mL can) for crushed
pineapple.*

Serving Suggestion

*A good lunch muffin to accompany
a fruit, melon, or avocado salad.*

Combine wet and dry mixtures and fold together gently until just mixed. Spoon into prepared pan. Bake at 400°F (200°C) for 20 to 25 minutes. Remove from pan and cool on rack.

yummy!

PUMPKIN

MAKES 12 MEDIUM

Preheat oven to 400°F (200°C) and prepare pan.

IN LARGE BOWL ADD AND COMBINE WELL

1 egg
⅔ cup (125 g) brown sugar
⅓ cup (75 g) butter or margarine, melted
¾ cup (175 mL) milk
¾ cup (175 mL) canned pumpkin
½ cup (85 g) raisins

♥

IN SMALLER BOWL COMBINE WELL

2 cups (280 g) all-purpose flour
2 tsp. baking powder
½ tsp. baking soda
½ tsp. salt
½ tsp. ground cinnamon
½ tsp. ground nutmeg
¼ tsp. ground ginger

Variation

Add roasted pumpkin seeds to batter and sprinkle additional seeds on top of each muffin.

Serving Suggestion

Try with Orange Cream Cheese Spread. *Make* Orange Butter *(see* Citrus *muffin); cream equal quantities of cream cheese and* Orange Butter *until light and fluffy.*

PUMPKIN ORANGE

MAKES 12 MEDIUM

*Preheat oven to 400°F (200°C)
and prepare pan.*

IN LARGE BOWL ADD AND COMBINE WELL

2 eggs
¾ cup (150 g) sugar
¼ cup (60 mL) oil
½ cup (125 mL) apple juice or cider
1 cup (240 mL) canned pumpkin
grated rind of 1 orange

♥

IN SMALLER BOWL COMBINE WELL

2 cups (280 g) all-purpose flour
1 Tbsp. baking powder
½ tsp. baking soda
½ tsp. salt
¼ tsp. ground cinnamon
¼ tsp. mace
⅛ tsp. ground cloves
½ cup chopped walnuts or pecans

Combine wet and dry mixtures and fold together gently until just mixed. Spoon into prepared pan and decorate top of each muffin with a walnut or pecan half. Bake at 400°F (200°C) for 20 to 25 minutes. Remove from pan and cool on rack.

Combine wet and dry mixtures and fold together gently until just mixed. Spoon into prepared pan. Bake at 375°C (190°C) for 25 minutes. Remove from pan and cool on rack.

Variation

RHUBARB ORANGE   *Add 1 tsp. grated orange peel. Substitute ¼ tsp. mace for cinnamon.*

Hint

Only fresh rhubarb will do; frozen rhubarb is often stringy and produces a soggy batter.

Serving Suggestion

Serve warm with stewed fruit and Cinnamon Butter *(see* Apple Plus *muffin), or dip hot muffin tops in melted butter and* Orange Sugar *(see* Citrus *muffin).*

RHUBARB CINNAMON

MAKES 12 MEDIUM

Preheat oven to 375°F (190°C) and prepare pan.

IN LARGE BOWL ADD AND COMBINE WELL

2 eggs
1 cup (190 g) sugar
¼ cup (60 mL) oil
½ cup (125 mL) plain yogurt
or buttermilk
1 tsp. vanilla
1¾ cups (200 g) chopped fresh
rhubarb, lightly packed

♥

IN SMALLER BOWL COMBINE WELL

2 cups (280 g) all-purpose flour
2 tsp. baking powder
½ tsp. baking soda
½ tsp. salt
¼ tsp. ground cinnamon

RICE

MAKES 12 MEDIUM

*Preheat oven to 400°F (200°C)
and prepare pan.*

IN LARGE BOWL ADD AND COMBINE WELL

1 egg
¼ cup (50 mL) honey
2 Tbsp. oil
½ cup (125 mL) milk
1 tsp. vanilla
1 cup (70 g) cooked rice,
    lightly packed

♥

IN SMALLER BOWL COMBINE WELL

1 cup (140 g) all-purpose flour
1 Tbsp. baking powder
½ tsp. baking soda
½ tsp. salt

*Combine wet and dry
mixtures and fold together
gently until just mixed.
Spoon into prepared pan
and decorate top of each
muffin with a walnut or
pecan half. Bake at 400°F
(200°C) for 15 to 20 minutes.
Remove from pan and cool
on rack.*

Variation

BROWN RICE   *Substitute cooked
brown rice for white.*

Hint

*Rice muffins should be eaten freshly
baked as rice dries out when frozen.*

Serving Suggestion

*A tasty luncheon accompaniment to
chicken salad or cold stuffed tomato.
Serve for breakfast with* Apple
Cinnamon Topping—*slice an apple
thinly, toss in cinnamon sugar. Press
two or three apple slices on tops of
each muffin before baking.*

Combine wet and dry mixtures and fold together gently until just mixed. Spoon into prepared pan. Bake at 400°F (200°C) for 20 minutes. Remove from pan and cool on rack.

Variation

RUM 'N' EGGNOG *Substitute ½ cup (70 g) commercial or homemade eggnog for milk, or dissolve 3 Tbsp. eggnog crystals in ½ cup (125 mL) milk.*

Hint

You may substitute 1 tsp. rum extract for vanilla, omit rum liquor and change milk to ¾ cup (175 mL).

RUM 'N' RAISIN

MAKES 8 MEDIUM

Preheat oven to 400°F (200°C) and prepare pan.

IN LARGE BOWL ADD AND COMBINE WELL

1 egg
⅓ cup (60 g) sugar
½ cup (115 g) butter, melted
½ cup (125 mL) milk
¼ cup (60 mL) light rum
1 tsp. vanilla
½ cup (85 g) raisins

♥

IN SMALLER BOWL COMBINE WELL

1¾ cups (240 g) cake flour
1½ tsp. baking powder
½ tsp. baking soda
¼ tsp. salt
¼ tsp. ground nutmeg

SESAME SEED

MAKES 12 MEDIUM

Preheat oven to 400°F (200°C) and prepare pan.

IN LARGE BOWL ADD AND COMBINE WELL

2 eggs
½ cup (125 mL) honey
¼ cup (60 mL) oil
⅔ cup (150 mL) milk
1 tsp. vanilla or ½ tsp. almond extract

♥

IN SMALLER BOWL COMBINE WELL

1 cup (140 g) cake flour
1 cup (115 g) ground sesame seeds
1½ tsp. baking powder
½ tsp. baking soda
½ tsp. salt
⅔ cup (115 g) raw sesame seeds

Combine wet and dry mixtures and fold together gently until just mixed. Spoon into prepared pan. Bake at 400°F (200°C) for 20 to 25 minutes. Remove from pan and cool on rack.

Variations

SUNFLOWER SEED *Substitute 1 cup (115 g) ground sunflower seeds for ground sesame seeds, and ½ cup (85 g) whole sunflower seeds for sesame seeds.*
SUNFLOWER OR SESAME DATE *Reduce honey to ¼ cup (50 mL). Add ½ cup (85 g) finely chopped dates to wet mixture.*

Serving Suggestion

Make Honey Orange Butter—*Cream ½ cup (115 g) unsalted butter together with ½ cup (125 mL) honey and the grated rind of one orange (approx. 1½ Tbsp.). When serving* Honey Orange Butter, *you may wish to reduce honey to ¼ cup (50 mL) in the muffin.*

Opposite: Sesame Seed Muffins with Orange Honey Butter

Prepare as shown at right, then take a portion of the batter and gently stir in dried fruits or nuts in whatever quantity you wish. Spoon into prepared pans. Bake at 375°F (190°C) for 20 minutes. Let cool a few minutes for easier removal. Remove from pans and cool on rack.

Variations

BRAN OATMEAL   *Substitute 4 cups (340 g) quick-cooking or old-fashioned oatmeal for All-Bran or Bran Buds cereal.*
BRAN AND GRAPE NUT CEREAL
Substitute 2 cups (175 g) Grape Nut flakes for bran flakes.
MOLASSES BRAN   *Substitute ½ cup (125 mL) unsulphured molasses plus 1½ cups (275 g) brown sugar for sugar.*

Hint

Keep batter in air-tight containers in refrigerator and fold in fruits and nuts just before baking.

SIX-WEEK REFRIGERATOR BRAN

MAKES 48 MEDIUM
Preheat oven to 375°F (190°C) and prepare pans.

MIX AND ALLOW TO COOL
2 cups (175 g) 100% bran flakes
2 cups (425 mL) boiling water

♥

IN LARGE BOWL CREAM WITH AN ELECTRIC MIXER
2 cups (450 g) margarine
2 cups (380 g) brown sugar or white
5 eggs

♥

IN SMALLER BOWL COMBINE WELL
5 cups (700 g) all-purpose flour
2 Tbsp. baking soda
½ tsp. salt

♥

ADD FLOUR MIXTURE TO CREAMED MIXTURE ALTERNATELY WITH
1 quart (950 mL) buttermilk

♥

GENTLY FOLD IN
bran mixture as prepared above
4 cups (340 g) All-Bran
or Bran Buds cereal

SOUR CREAM COFFEE

MAKES 12 MEDIUM

Preheat oven to 375°F (190°C) and prepare pan.

MAKE FILLING BY RUBBING TOGETHER

¼ cup (40 g) brown sugar
¼ cup (30 g) finely chopped walnuts
or pecans
½ tsp. ground cinnamon

♥

IN LARGE BOWL CREAM WITH
ELECTRIC MIXER

½ cup (115 g) butter
½ cup (85 g) sugar
2 eggs

♥

ADD AND COMBINE WELL

1 cup (240 mL) sour cream
1 tsp. vanilla

♥

IN SMALLER BOWL COMBINE WELL

2 cups (280 g) all-purpose flour
1 tsp. baking powder
1 tsp. baking soda
¼ tsp. salt

Combine wet and dry mixtures and fold together gently until just mixed. Spoon 1 Tbsp. batter into each cup. Sprinkle 1 tsp. filling in the middle of each muffin. Top with 1 Tbsp. batter. Sprinkle remaining filling on top of each muffin. Bake at 375°F (190°C) for 25 minutes. Remove from pan and cool on rack.

Hint

Calorie watchers—replace sour cream with non-fat plain yogurt.

Make a sweet potato purée by draining 1 14-oz. (398-mL) can of sweet potato and purée in blender or food processor. Set aside.

Combine wet and dry mixtures and fold together gently until just mixed. Spoon into prepared pan and decorate top of each muffin with a walnut or pecan half. Bake at 400°F (200°C) for 20 minutes. Remove from pan and cool on rack.

Variation

SWEET POTATO ORANGE
Substitute the grated rind of 1 orange (approx. 1½ Tbsp.) for vanilla.

Serving Suggestions

Serve instead of dinner roll at buffet meal or barbecue. Try with ham, spareribs or sausages. Or make a Melted Marshmallow Topping—just 5 minutes before baking is completed, place one large marshmallow on top of each muffin. Return to oven for 5 minutes.

SWEET POTATO

MAKES 15 MEDIUM

Preheat oven to 400°F (200°C) and prepare pan.

IN LARGE BOWL ADD AND COMBINE WELL

3 eggs
⅔ cup (125 g) lightly packed brown sugar
½ cup (115 g) butter or margarine, melted
1¼ cups (300 mL) prepared sweet potato purée
½ cup (125 mL) milk
½ tsp. vanilla

♥

IN SMALLER BOWL COMBINE WELL

2 cups (280 g) all-purpose flour
2 tsp. baking powder
½ tsp. baking soda
½ tsp. salt
¼ tsp. ground nutmeg
one pinch ground cloves
½ cup (60 g) chopped walnuts or pecans

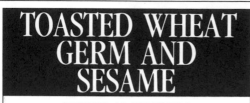

TOASTED WHEAT GERM AND SESAME

MAKES 10 MEDIUM

Preheat oven to 400°F (200°C) and prepare pan.

IN LARGE BOWL ADD AND COMBINE WELL

2 eggs
½ cup (85 g) brown sugar
½ cup (125 mL) oil
1 tsp. vanilla or ½ tsp. maple extract

♥

IN SMALLER BOWL COMBINE WELL

1 cup (140 g) cake flour
1 cup (85 g) toasted wheat germ
2 tsp. baking powder
½ tsp. baking soda
½ tsp. salt
¼ cup (40 g) raw sesame seeds

Combine wet and dry mixtures and fold together gently until just mixed. Spoon into prepared pan. Bake at 400°F (200°C) for 20 to 25 minutes. Remove from pan and cool on rack.

Variation

GRAHAM CRACKER *Omit sesame seeds and substitute graham cracker crumbs for toasted wheat germ. Reduce brown sugar to ¼ cup (40 g).*

Serving Suggestion

Make Lemon *or* Orange Cream Cheese Spread—*see* Citrus Zucchini/ Courgette *or* Pumpkin.

Combine wet and dry mixtures and fold together gently until just mixed. Spoon into prepared pan. Bake at 400°F (200°C) for 20 to 25 minutes. Remove from pan and cool on rack.

Variation

CRACKED WHEAT *Substitute ¾ cup (85 g) cracked wheat for Twelve-grain cereal.*

Hint

The twelve grains are cracked wheat, rye meal, cornmeal, rolled oats, barley grits, sunflower seeds, sesame seeds, buckwheat groats, flaxseed, millet, rice grits, and soya grits. Six-grain cereal is also available and may be substituted.

TWELVE-GRAIN

MAKES 12 MEDIUM

Preheat oven to 400°F (200°C) and prepare pan.

COMBINE AND ALLOW TO COOL

¾ cup (85 g) Twelve-grain cereal
1½ cups (350 mL) boiling water
1 tsp. instant coffee (optional)

♥

IN LARGE BOWL ADD AND COMBINE WELL

1 egg
¼ cup (40 g) brown sugar
½ cup (125 mL) oil
Twelve-grain mixture
as prepared above
1 tsp. vanilla or maple extract
¾ cup (125 g) chopped dates

♥

IN SMALLER BOWL COMBINE WELL

1½ cups (210 g) cake flour
2 tsp. baking powder
½ tsp. baking soda
½ tsp. salt

WHOLE-WHEAT

MAKES 10 MEDIUM

*Preheat oven to 375°F (190°C)
and prepare pan.*

IN LARGE BOWL ADD AND COMBINE WELL

2 eggs
¼ cup (60 mL) honey
½ cup (125 mL) oil
¾ cup (175 mL) milk
1 tsp. vanilla

♥

IN SMALLER BOWL COMBINE WELL

1 cup (140 g) whole-wheat flour
½ cup (70 g) cake flour
1½ tsp. baking powder
½ tsp. baking soda
½ tsp. salt

*Combine wet and dry
mixtures and fold together
until just mixed. Spoon into
prepared pan. Bake at 375°F
(190°C) for 20 to 25 minutes.*

Variation

WHOLE-WHEAT MOLASSES
*Substitute 2 Tbsp. unsulphured
molasses and 2 Tbsp. honey for
¼ cup (60 mL) honey.*

Serving Suggestion

Make Sunflower Seed Spread—
*Cream together until light and fluffy
1 cup (140 g) ground raw sunflower
seeds, ¼ cup (60 mL) peanut butter,
2 Tbsp. sunflower seed oil, ¼ tsp.
seasoned salt.*

Combine wet and dry mixtures and fold together gently until just mixed. Spoon into prepared pan. Bake at 400°F (200°C) for 20 to 25 minutes. Remove from pan and cool on rack.

Variations

WHOLE-WHEAT BLUEBERRY ORANGE *Substitute whole fresh or frozen blueberries for cranberries.*
PLAIN CRANBERRY OR BLUEBERRY ORANGE *Substitute 1 cup (140 g) all-purpose flour plus 1¼ cup (175 g) cake flour for whole-wheat flour.*

Hint

Do not defrost frozen blueberries or cranberries before using. Defrosted berries produce a highly discolored batter.

Serving Suggestion

Make miniatures for holiday parties. Freezes well. Makes attractive Christmas gift.

WHOLE-WHEAT CRANBERRY ORANGE

MAKES 24 MINIATURE OR 12 MEDIUM

Preheat oven to 400°F (200°C) and prepare pan.

IN LARGE BOWL ADD AND COMBINE WELL

2 eggs
½–¾ cup (85–150 g) brown sugar
½ cup (125 mL) oil
1 cup (240 mL) milk
grated rind of 1 orange

♥

IN SMALLER BOWL COMBINE WELL

2 cups (280 g) whole-wheat flour
1 Tbsp. baking powder
½ tsp. baking soda
½ tsp. salt
1½ cups (350 g) chopped frozen or fresh cranberries

WHOLE-WHEAT PEACH

MAKES 12 MEDIUM

*Preheat oven to 375°F (190°C)
and prepare pan.*

IN LARGE BOWL ADD AND COMBINE WELL

4 eggs
½ cup (85 g) brown sugar
⅓ cup (75 mL) oil
¾ cup (175 mL) milk
1 cup (240 ml) chopped
canned peaches, well drained
(1 14-oz. or 398-mL can)
½ tsp almond extract

♥

IN SMALLER BOWL COMBINE WELL

1 cup (140 g) whole-wheat flour
1 cup (140 g) cake flour
1 Tbsp. baking powder
1 tsp. baking soda
¼ tsp. salt
½ cup (60 g) chopped almonds
or pecans

*Combine wet and dry
mixtures and fold together
gently until just mixed.
Spoon into prepared pan
and decorate top of each
muffin with an almond or
pecan half. Bake at 375°F
(190°C) for 25 to 30 minutes.
Remove from pan and cool
on rack.*

Variations

WHOLE-WHEAT APRICOT
*Substitute 1 cup (175 g) chopped
canned apricots (1 14-oz. or 398-mL
can) for peaches.*
**WHOLE-WHEAT PEACH OR
APRICOT WITH COCONUT**
*Reduce cake flour to ½ cup (70 g)
and add ½ cup (60 g) unsweetened
shredded coconut to dry mixture.*
WHOLE-WHEAT PEAR GINGER
*Substitute 1 cup (115 g) canned
chopped pears for peaches. Omit
almond extract and add 6 to 8
pieces of finely chopped crystallized
ginger to dry mixture.*

Combine wet and dry mixtures and fold together gently until just mixed. Spoon into prepared pan and decorate top of each muffin with a walnut or pecan half. Bake at 400°F (200°C) for 20 to 25 minutes. Remove from pan and cool on rack.

Variations

CARROT SPICE *Substitute 1½ cups (210 g) finely grated carrot for zucchini/courgette. Add ½ cup (85 g) raisins.*
WHOLE-WHEAT CARROT OR ZUCCHINI/COURGETTE *Substitute 1 cup (140 g) whole-wheat flour and ½ cup (70 g) cake flour for 1½ cups (210 g) all-purpose flour.*

Serving Suggestion

Make Cream Cheese Spread—Mix equal quantities of butter and cream cheese. Whip until light and fluffy.

ZUCCHINI/ COURGETTE SPICE

MAKES 10 MEDIUM
Preheat oven to 400°F (200°C) and prepare pan.

IN LARGE BOWL ADD AND COMBINE WELL

2 eggs
⅔ cup (125 g) brown sugar
½ cup (125 mL) oil
¼ cup (60 mL) milk
1 tsp. vanilla
1½ cups (210 g) grated unpeeled zucchini/courgette

♥

IN SMALLER BOWL COMBINE WELL

1½ cups (210 g) all-purpose flour
1½ tsp. baking powder
½ tsp. baking soda
½ tsp. salt
½ tsp. ground cinnamon
¼ tsp. ground nutmeg
½ cup (60 g) chopped walnuts or pecans

73

SAVORY MUFFINS

CARAWAY CHEESE

MAKES 12 MEDIUM

Preheat oven to 400°F (200°C) and prepare pan.

IN LARGE BOWL ADD AND COMBINE WELL

2 eggs
¼ cup (40 g) sugar
¼ cup (60 mL) oil
¾ cup (175 mL) plain yogurt
or buttermilk
1 cup (240 mL) creamed
cottage cheese
1½ tsp. caraway seeds, or to taste
1 tsp. grated lemon rind

♥

IN SMALLER BOWL COMBINE WELL

1 cup (140 g) whole-wheat flour
1 cup (140 g) cake flour
2 tsp. baking powder
½ tsp. baking soda
½ tsp. salt

Combine wet and dry mixtures and fold together gently until just mixed. Spoon into prepared pan. Bake at 400°F (200°C) for 20 to 25 minutes. Remove from pan and cool on rack.

Variation

POPPY SEED CHEESE *Substitute 1 1/2 tsp. poppy seeds for caraway seeds.*

Serving Suggestion

Make Cream Cheese Spread *(see* Zucchini/Courgette Spice *muffin).*

Combine wet and dry mixtures and fold together gently until just mixed. Spoon into prepared pan and sprinkle a small amount of caraway seed on each muffin top. Bake at 400°F (200°C) for 20 to 25 minutes. Remove from pan and cool on rack.

Variation

DILL ONION *Substitute dill seed for caraway.*

Serving Suggestion

Goes well with potato soup and fish.

CARAWAY ONION

MAKES 12 MEDIUM

Preheat oven to 400°F (200°C) and prepare pan.

IN A LARGE FRYING PAN SAUTÉ IN BACON FAT OR OIL UNTIL GOLDEN, THEN COOL

¼ cup (60 mL) bacon fat or oil
½ cup (60 g) finely chopped onion
1½ tsp. caraway seeds, or to taste

♥

IN A LARGE BOWL ADD AND COMBINE WELL

1 egg
¼ cup (60 mL) unsulphured molasses
1 cup (240 mL) milk
onion mixture as prepared above

♥

IN SMALLER BOWL COMBINE WELL

1 cup (140 g) whole-wheat flour
1 cup (140 g) all-purpose flour
1 Tbsp. baking powder
½ tsp. baking soda
1 tsp. salt

CARAWAY RYE

MAKES 10 MEDIUM

***Preheat oven to 400°F (200°C)
and prepare pan.***

IN LARGE BOWL ADD AND COMBINE WELL

1 egg
2 Tbsp. brown sugar
¼ cup (60 mL) oil
1 cup (240 mL) milk
1 cup (150 g) rye flakes
¾ tsp. caraway seeds, or to taste

♥

IN SMALLER BOWL COMBINE WELL

1 cup (140 g) all-purpose flour
2 tsp. baking powder
½ tsp. salt

*Combine wet and dry
mixtures and fold together
gently until just mixed.
Spoon into prepared pan.
Bake at 400°F (200°C) for 20
minutes. Remove from pan
and cool on rack.*

Hint

*Rye flakes are available in natural
foods stores.*

Serving Suggestion

Spread with whipped cream cheese.

Plain Rye *is very tasty with* Parmesan
Butter—*Cream together until light
and fluffy ½ cup (115 g) softened
butter, ½ cup (60 g) grated
Parmesan cheese, 2 Tbsp. chopped
fresh parsley, and ½ tsp. onion
powder.*

Combine wet and dry mixtures and fold together gently until just mixed. Spoon into prepared pan. Bake at 400°F (200°C) for 20 minutes. Remove from pan and cool on rack.

Serving Suggestion

Make Parmesan Butter *(see* Caraway Rye Flake *muffin) and serve with cream of tomato soup or serve warm with meatloaf.*

CELERY

MAKES 12 MEDIUM

Preheat oven to 400°F (200°C) and prepare pan.

IN LARGE BOWL ADD AND COMBINE WELL

4 eggs
½ cup (125 mL) oil
1 10-oz. (284-mL) can cream of celery soup
1 cup (115 g) chopped celery
¼ cup (30 g) grated Parmesan cheese
2 Tbsp. freshly chopped parsley
¼ tsp. celery salt
¼ tsp. onion salt

♥

IN SMALLER BOWL COMBINE WELL

2 cups (280 g) all-purpose flour
2 tsp. baking powder
1 tsp. baking soda

Combine wet and dry mixtures and fold together gently until just mixed. Spoon into prepared pan. Bake at 400°F (200°C) for 20 to 25 minutes. Remove from pan and cool on rack.

CHEESE WITH PARSLEY AND PEPPERS

MAKES 12 MEDIUM

Preheat oven to 400°F (200°C) and prepare pan.

IN LARGE BOWL ADD AND COMBINE WELL

2 eggs
½ cup (125 mL) oil
1 10-oz. (284-mL) can condensed cheddar cheese soup
⅓ cup (40 g) chopped green pepper
½ cup (15 g) chopped fresh parsley
4 dashes Worcestershire sauce

♥

IN SMALLER BOWL COMBINE WELL

1 cup (140 g) whole-wheat flour
1 cup (140 g) cake flour
1 Tbsp. baking powder
¼ tsp. baking soda
½ tsp. salt or seasoned salt

Variation

CHEESE WITH PARSLEY AND ONION *Substitute 2 Tbsp. dried parsley and 2 Tbsp. dried onion flakes for fresh parsley and peppers.*

Hint

Before baking, place a small piece of cheese on each muffin top for extra cheese flavor.

Serving Suggestion

Excellent accompaniment for a variety of soups—cream of chicken or potato, gazpacho, tomato, or minestrone. Try serving with chili con carne.

Opposite: Cheese Muffins with Parsley & Peppers

Combine wet and dry mixtures and fold together gently until just mixed. Spoon into prepared pan. Bake at 400°F (200°C) for 20 minutes. Remove from pan and cool on rack.

CHEESE 'N' V-8

MAKES 10 MEDIUM

Preheat oven to 400°F (200°C) and prepare pan.

IN LARGE BOWL ADD AND COMBINE WELL

1 egg
⅓ cup (75 mL) oil
1 cup (240 mL) V-8 juice
½ cup (60 g) grated sharp Cheddar

♥

IN SMALLER BOWL COMBINE WELL

1¾ cup (175 g) all-purpose flour
2 tsp. baking powder
½ tsp. baking soda
½ tsp. salt

Serving Suggestion

Serve with a salad and quiche or omelette for lunch. This muffin adds zest to bland soups such as cream of celery, mushroom, or potato.

CORN NIBLET

MAKES 12 MEDIUM

*Preheat oven to 400°F (200°C)
and prepare pan.*

IN LARGE BOWL ADD AND COMBINE WELL

2 eggs

½ cup (115 g) butter or margarine,
melted

1½ cups (350 mL) buttermilk

1 cup (175 g) cornmeal

1 cup (175 g) whole kernel corn
(1 12-oz. (375-mL) can)

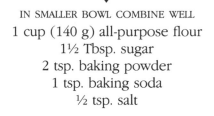

IN SMALLER BOWL COMBINE WELL

1 cup (140 g) all-purpose flour

1½ Tbsp. sugar

2 tsp. baking powder

1 tsp. baking soda

½ tsp. salt

Combine wet and dry mixtures and fold together gently until just mixed. Spoon into prepared pan. Bake at 400°F (200°C) for 25 minutes. Remove from pan and cool on rack.

Variation

BACON CORN NIBLET   *Omit salt. Chop 10 slices of bacon, fry until crisp, and set aside. Pour bacon fat into measuring cup and add oil to measure ½ cup (125 mL). Put into wet mixture. Fold bacon into batter at last moment.*

Serving Suggestion

Good with eggs, ham, or chicken. Take to a potluck supper instead of rolls.

Spoon into prepared pan. Bake at 400°F (200°C) for 20 minutes. Remove from pan and cool on rack.

ALL CORN

MAKES 10 MEDIUM

Preheat oven to 400°F (200°C) and prepare pan.

IN LARGE BOWL ADD AND COMBINE WELL

1 cup (175 g) cornmeal
2 tsp. baking powder
½ tsp. baking soda
1 tsp. salt

♥

ADD AND COMBINE WELL

2 eggs
¼ cup (60 mL) corn oil
1 cup (240 mL) sour cream
1 cup (240 mL) creamed corn

Hint

Only one bowl is required as there is no flour to incorporate.

Serving Suggestions

Serve with bacon or sausages for breakfast, or with ham or chicken for dinner. Excellent with cream of tomato soup.

CORNMEAL SAGE

MAKES 14 MEDIUM

*Preheat oven to 400°F (200°C)
and prepare pan.*

MIX AND ALLOW TO SOAK FOR 10 MINUTES

1½ cups (250 g) cornmeal
2 cups (425 mL) buttermilk

♥

IN LARGE BOWL ADD AND COMBINE WELL

3 eggs
1 Tbsp. sugar
½ cup (115 g) butter or margarine,
melted
1 Tbsp. fresh or 1 tsp. dried sage

♥

IN SMALLER BOWL COMBINE WELL

1½ cups (210 g) all-purpose flour
1 Tbsp. baking powder
1 tsp. baking soda
1½ tsp. salt

*Combine wet and dry
mixtures and fold together
gently until just mixed.
Spoon into prepared pan.
Bake at 400°F (200°C) for 20
minutes. Remove from pan
and cool on rack.*

Variation

CORNMEAL MARJORAM   *Substitute
1 Tbsp. fresh marjoram or 1 tsp.
dried for sage.*

Serving Suggestions

*With ground beef casserole, roast
chicken, or a hearty stew.*

Combine wet and dry mixtures and fold together gently until just mixed. Spoon into prepared pan. Bake at 400°F (200°C) for 25 minutes. Remove from pan and cool on rack.

Variation

CORNMEAL WITH TOMATO BITS
Substitute 1¼ cups (300 mL) milk for canned tomatoes. Reduce oil to ¼ cup (60 mL) and add 1 cup (175 g) peeled, seeded chopped fresh tomatoes to wet mixture.

Hint

For best flavor, muffin must be served very warm with butter. Use only fresh tomatoes in season for variation.

Serving Suggestion

Try with clam or fish chowder.

CORNMEAL TOMATO

MAKES 12 MEDIUM
Preheat oven to 400°F (200°C) and prepare pan.

COMBINE AND LET SOAK FOR **10** MINUTES
1 cup (175 g) cornmeal
1 14-oz. (398-mL) can canned tomatoes, including liquid

♥

IN LARGE BOWL ADD AND COMBINE WELL
2 eggs
2 Tbsp. brown sugar
½ cup (125 mL) oil
cornmeal mixture as prepared above
¾ tsp. dried sweet basil, or to taste

♥

IN SMALLER BOWL COMBINE WELL
1½ cups (210 g) all-purpose flour
1 Tbsp. baking powder
½ tsp. baking soda
1 tsp. salt
¼ tsp. garlic powder

COTTAGE CHEESE DILL

MAKES 12 MEDIUM

Preheat oven to 400°F (200°C) and prepare pan.

IN LARGE BOWL ADD AND COMBINE WELL

1 egg
¼ cup (60 mL) oil
½ cup (125 mL) milk
1 cup (240 mL) small-curd creamed
cottage cheese
2 Tbsp. finely chopped fresh
young dill
2 Tbsp. chopped green onion
½ tsp. Worcestershire sauce
½ tsp. seasoned salt

♥

IN SMALLER BOWL COMBINE WELL

2 cups (280 g) all-purpose flour
1 Tbsp. baking powder

Combine wet and dry mixtures and fold together gently until just mixed. Spoon into prepared pan. Bake at 400°F (200°C) for 25 to 30 minutes. Remove from pan and cool on rack.

Variation

POTATO WITH DILL-ONION-PARSLEY *Substitute 1 10-oz. (284-mL) can of cream of potato soup for cheese and purée in blender or food processor. Add 2 Tbsp. chopped fresh parsley to wet mixture.*

Serving Suggestion

Good with fresh asparagus or tomato soup, or serve for brunch with scrambled eggs and corned beef hash.

Combine wet and dry mixtures and fold together gently until just mixed. Spoon into prepared pan. Bake at 400°F (200°C) for 20 minutes. Remove from pan and cool on rack.

Variation

KERNEL CORN CHEESE *Substitute 1 cup (115 g) whole kernel corn (drained) for creamed corn. Substitute 1 cup (240 mL) buttermilk for sour cream.*

Hint

To grate fresh cheese more easily, first freeze for 30 to 40 minutes.

Serving Suggestion

A fast supper when served with fried sausages and bean salad.

CREAMY CORN CHEESE

MAKES 12 MEDIUM

Preheat oven to 400°F (200°C) and prepare pan.

IN LARGE BOWL ADD AND COMBINE WELL

1 egg
¼ cup (60 mL) corn oil
¼ cup (60 mL) sour cream
1¼ cups (300 mL) creamed corn
(1 10-oz. (284-mL) can)
¾ cup (85 g) grated sharp
or medium cheddar

♥

IN SMALLER BOWL COMBINE WELL

1½ cups (210 g) all-purpose flour
1 Tbsp. sugar
1½ tsp. baking powder
½ tsp. baking soda
½ tsp. salt

HAM NUGGET IN CORN

MAKES 12 MEDIUM

*Preheat oven to 400°F (200°C)
and prepare pan.*

IN LARGE BOWL ADD AND COMBINE WELL

2 eggs
½ cup (125 mL) oil
1½ cups (350 mL) creamed corn
(1 14-oz. (398-mL) can)

♥

IN SMALLER BOWL COMBINE WELL

1 cup (140 g) whole-wheat flour
1 cup (140 g) all-purpose flour
1 Tbsp. baking powder
½ tsp. salt
12 ½-inch cubes of ham

*Combine wet and dry
mixtures and fold together
gently until just mixed.
Spoon into prepared pan
and press one ½-inch cube
of ham into center of each
muffin. Bake at 400°F
(200°C) for 20 to 25 minutes.
Remove from pan and cool
on rack.*

Variation

CHEDDAR NUGGET IN CORN
Substitute cubes of cheddar for ham.

Hint

Eat Cheddar Nugget in Corn *muffin
warm and freshly baked. Melted
cheddar cheese becomes tough when
cooled.*

Serving Suggestion

*Children enjoy finding the "nugget."
Chicken noodle soup goes well with
these muffins.*

Opposite: Cornmeal Muffins with Tomato Bits (p. 85)

Combine wet and dry mixtures and fold together gently until just mixed. Spoon into prepared pan. Bake at 400°F (200°C) for 20 minutes. Remove from pan and cool on rack.

Hint

Snip fresh parsley, dill, chives, or other fresh herbs with kitchen shears.

Serving Suggestion

Make Cheddar Butter—Cream together until light and fluffy ½ cup (115 g) softened butter, ½ cup (60 g) grated mild or medium cheddar cheese, 2 Tbsp. chopped fresh parsley.

ONION PARSLEY

MAKES 12 MEDIUM

Preheat oven to 400°F (200°C) and prepare pan.

IN LARGE BOWL ADD AND COMBINE WELL

1 egg
¼ cup (60 mL) oil
1 cup (240 mL) milk
⅓ cup (40 g) finely chopped green onion
⅓ cup (10 g) finely chopped fresh parsley

IN SMALLER BOWL COMBINE WELL

2 cups (280 g) all-purpose flour
1 Tbsp. sugar
1 Tbsp. baking powder
1½ tsp. salt

PARMESAN

MAKES 12 MEDIUM

*Preheat oven to 400°F (200°C)
and prepare pan.*

IN LARGE BOWL ADD AND COMBINE WELL

2 eggs
½ cup (125 mL) oil
¾ cup (175 mL) milk

♥

IN SMALLER BOWL COMBINE WELL

1 cup (140 g) whole-wheat flour
1 cup (140 g) cake flour
½ cup (60 g) grated Parmesan cheese
1 Tbsp. sugar
1 Tbsp. baking powder
½ tsp. garlic salt
½ tsp. onion salt

Combine wet and dry mixtures and fold together gently until just mixed. Spoon into prepared pan. Bake at 400°F (200°C) for 20 to 25 minutes. Remove from pan and cool on rack.

Variation

ZUCCHINI/COURGETTE PARMESAN
Reduce milk to ¼ cup (60 mL). Add 1 cup (150 g) freshly grated zucchini/courgette, unpeeled, to wet mixture.

Hint

Use good quality Parmesan.

Serving Suggestion

Goes well with salads or Italian dishes.

GLOSSARY

Carob
A chocolate substitute, available in health food stores. Available in powder or chip form. When substituting for chocolate, use less sugar.

Chocolate/Cocoa
Chocolate for baking is available as unsweetened or bitter chocolate, semi-sweet or bitter-sweet, and sweetened solid chocolate bars. Cocoa is a powder and in its pure form is unsweetened. Do not substitute instant cocoa, which is precooked and sweetened.

Flour
Wheat flours can be categorized as hard or soft, depending on gluten content. Gluten is a protein substance which helps flour rise during baking. Low-gluten flours should be combined with high-gluten flours for best results, or use all-purpose flour, which is a blend of hard and soft flours. The flour measurements in this book are for unsifted flour. Measure flour straight from package. Non-wheat flours have no gluten and require more leavening than wheat flours. They should be combined with wheat flours for best results. Types of flour:

- *All-purpose. A blend of hard and soft wheats, usually with a high gluten content.*
- *Barley. Finely milled kernel of barley, much like rye flour in texture and moistness.*
- *Bread. A high-gluten wheat flour, not suitable for muffin-baking.*
- *Cake. A finely milled soft wheat flour with a low gluten content. Whole-wheat cake flour is also available.*
- *Farina. Made from durum wheat after the germ and bran have been removed.*
- *Gluten. A high-protein hard wheat flour with most of the starch removed.*
- *Graham. A type of whole-wheat flour in which the bran is coarsely ground.*
- *Instant. Ground to a powder and gives a different texture to baking. Not suitable for muffins.*
- *Rye. A heavy flour with low gluten content.*
- *Self-rising. Contains baking powder. 1 cup (140 g) self-rising flour equals 1 cup (140 g) all-purpose plus 1 teaspoon baking powder.*
- *Semolina. Made from hard wheat durum flour.*
- *Triticale. A cross between rye and wheat, with rye flavor.*
- *Unbleached. A slightly harder all-purpose flour. A mixture of ¾ cup (100 g) unbleached plus ¼ cup (35 g) cake flour equals 1 cup (140 g) all-purpose. Has shorter shelf life and should be refrigerated.*

• *Whole-wheat. Made from the kernel of the wheat and includes wheat germ and bran. Store in refrigerator.*

Milk powder
Instant, nonfat milk. Can be substituted for milk, but mix powder with dry ingredients.

Molasses
For optimum flavor, molasses should replace no more than half of the sweetening power in a recipe. There are three types of molasses:

• *Unsulphured. Manufactured from juice of sun-ripened cane.*
• *Sulphured. A by-product of sugar.*
• *Blackstrap. Waste product of sugar.*

Oils
There are nut oils and vegetable oils. Nut oils do not react well to heat and are not suitable for baking. Use vegetable oils pressed from corn, cottonseed, olive, soybean, sesame, sunflower, and safflower. Oils are 100 percent fat and should not be substituted measure for measure for butter. In substituting, adjust (e.g., 1/3 cup/75 g butter for 1/4 cup/ 60 ml oil). Vegetable shortening may be substituted for butter equally.

Wheat Germ
Made from the kernel of the wheat grain. Should be stored in refrigerator. Comes raw and toasted.

INDEX

FAVORITE RECIPES

FAVORITE RECIPES

FAVORITE RECIPES

FAVORITE RECIPES

FAVORITE RECIPES

FAVORITE RECIPES

FAVORITE RECIPES

FAVORITE RECIPES

Angela Clubb is a popular Canadian cookbook author. A self-taught cook, Angela lives in Burlington, Ontario, with her husband and two children. Wild About Muffins *is her first book, published originally in Canada; later books include* Mad About Cheddar *and* Fun in the Kitchen, *a cookbook for adults to use with children.*